Butterfly Visits

by Rebecca Sangueza

Illustrated by Holly Donelson

Published by Sangueza Publishing
sanguezapublishing@gmail.com
www.facebook.com/butterflyvisits
Text copyright © 2016 Rebecca Sangueza
Illustrations copyright © 2016 Holly Donelson
All rights reserved, inlcuding the right of reproduction, in whole or part, in any form.

ISBN 978-1-53735-572-6

Page design by Lily Donelson

Blessings,
Rebecca
Sangüeza

In loving memory of
Jose Antonio Sangueza
Dedicated son, husband, father, soldier and friend

Whose life touched so many in such significant ways

Have you ever wondered about butterflies and why they decide to visit us?

They have a whole flock of friends
who they travel with, and yet,
so many times you see them alone.

I feel something special when a butterfly decides to stop and visit. It is almost like the butterfly is delivering a message especially for me.

I have been places before – places I visited with someone who has died.

And, when I go to those places again,
a butterfly sometimes joins me.
I wonder if the butterfly is telling me something,
or sending me a special message
from someone who is now in heaven.

I wonder if the butterfly is telling me the person I miss is okay.

I wonder if it is God's way of showing me the person I miss is happy.

It is so fun to see the butterfly pause,
to move his wings and antennas,
as if he is talking to me.

The message is calming and peaceful.
It brings back the warm memories
of the person who died,
and also tells me things will be okay.
I am thankful for the butterfly's visit
and the comfort it brings.

Go butterfly, know I am well . . .
know I miss my loved one,
and that I am blessed to
have had a visit from you.

Thank you butterfly,

I hope you come to visit me again.

About the author

REBECCA REEVES SANGUEZA is a native Texan, former educator, coach and military wife. She received her BS in Education from Eastern New Mexico University and a MA in Mass Communications from Texas Tech University. She resides in Colorado Springs and is the mother of two young men who carry on the legacy of their father's love for the outdoors, with passions for fishing and mountain climbing.

About the illustrator

HOLLY DONELSON grew up surrounded and supported by a large extended family in the beautiful Berkshire Hills of Western Massachusetts. She and Rebecca met when their boys were in first grade, and they have shared many adventures together since. Holly received a BFA from the University of Massachusetts and has spent most of the last 20 years living in Colorado with her husband and children, where butterflies visit often.

Butterflies of the Rocky Mountain Region Used in This Book

MONARCH
Danaus plexippus

MELISSA BLUE
Plebjus melissa

WESTERN TIGER SWALLOWTAIL
Papilio rutulus

BLUE COPPER
Lycaena heteronea

LARGE MARBLE
Euchloe ausonides

Made in the USA
San Bernardino, CA
29 April 2017